Potatoes
Cassava
Carrots
Turnips
Beets
Radishes
Potatoes

PLANTS WE EAT

Cassava
Carrots
Turnips
Beets
Radishes
Potatoes
Cassava
Carrots
Turnips
Beets
Radishes
Potatoes
Cassava

Buried Treasure

Roots & Tubers

Meredith Sayles Hughes
and Tom Hughes

Lerner Publications Company/Minneapolis

Check out the authors' website at www.foodmuseum.com/hughes

Website address: www.lernerbooks.com

Designers: Steven P. Foley, Sean W. Todd
Editors: Domenica DiPiazza, Mary M. Rodgers
Photo Researcher: Daniel S. Mesnik

LIBRARY OF CONGRESS CATALOGING-IN-
PUBLICATION DATA

Hughes, Meredith Sayles.
    Buried treasure: roots & tubers / by Meredith Sayles
Hughes and Tom Hughes.
        p. cm. — (Plants we eat)
    Includes index.
    Summary: Relates the history and describes the use
and production of such roots and tubers as potatoes,
cassava, carrots, beets, turnips, and radishes. Includes
recipes.
    ISBN 0-8225-2830-4 (lib. bdg. : alk. paper)
    1. Root crops—Juvenile literature. 2. Tuber crops—
Juvenile literature. 3. Potatoes—Juvenile literature.
[1. Food crops. 2. Plants, Edible. 3. Potatoes.]
I. Hughes, E. Thomas, 1945– II. Title. III. Series.
SB209.H84 1998
635'.1—dc21   97-28436

Manufactured in the United States of America
1 2 3 4 5 6 – JR – 03 02 01 00 99 98

The glossary on page 77 gives definitions of
words shown in **bold type** in the text.

Contents

Introduction

Plants make all life on our planet possible. They provide the oxygen we breathe and the food we eat. Think about a burger and fries. The meat comes from cattle, which eat plants. The fries are potatoes cooked in oil from soybeans, corn, or sunflowers. The burger bun is a wheat product. Ketchup is a mixture of tomatoes, herbs, and corn syrup or the sugar from sugarcane. How about some onions or pickle relish with your burger?

How Plants Make Food

By snatching sunlight, water, and carbon dioxide from the atmosphere and mixing them together—a complex process called **photosynthesis**—green plants create food energy. The raw food energy is called glucose, a simple form of sugar. From this storehouse of glucose, each plant produces fats, carbohydrates, and proteins—the elements that make up the bulk of the foods humans and animals eat.

Sunlight peeks through the branches of a plant-covered tree in a tropical rain forest, where all the elements exist for photosynthesis to take place.

First we eat, then we do everything else.

— M. F. K. Fisher

Plants offer more than just food. They provide the raw materials for making the clothes you're wearing and the paper in books, magazines, and newspapers. Much of what's in your home comes from plants—the furniture, the wallpaper, and even the glue that holds the paper on the wall. Eons ago plants created the gas and oil we put in our cars, buses, and airplanes. Plants even give us the gum we chew.

On the Move

Although we don't think of plants as beings on the move, they have always been pioneers. From their beginnings as algaelike creatures in the sea to their movement onto dry land about 400 million years ago, plants have colonized new territories. Alone on the barren rock of the earliest earth, plants slowly established an environment so rich with food, shelter, and oxygen that some forms of marine life took up residence on dry land. Helped along by birds who scattered seeds far and wide, plants later sped up their travels, moving to cover most of our planet.

Early in human history, when few people lived on the earth, gathering food was everyone's main activity. Small family groups were nomadic, venturing into areas that offered a source of water, shelter, and foods such as fruits, nuts, seeds, and small game animals. After they had eaten up the region's food sources, the family group moved on to another spot. Only when people noticed that food plants were renewable—that the berry bushes would bear fruit again and that grasses gave forth seeds year after year—did family groups begin to settle in any one area for more than a single season.

Organisms that behave like algae—small, rootless plants that live in water

It's a Fact!

The term *photosynthesis* comes from Greek words meaning "putting together with light." This chemical process, which takes place in a plant's leaves, is part of the natural cycle that balances the earth's store of carbon dioxide and oxygen.

Native Americans were the first peoples to plant crops in North America.

Domestication of plants probably began as an accident. Seeds from a wild plant eaten at dinner were tossed onto a trash pile. Later a plant grew there, was eaten, and its seeds were tossed onto the pile. The cycle continued on its own until someone noticed the pattern and repeated it deliberately. Agriculture radically changed human life. From relatively small plots of land, more people could be fed over time, and fewer people were required to hunt and gather food. Diets shifted from a broad range of wild foods to a more limited but more consistent menu built around one main crop such as wheat, corn, cassava, rice, or potatoes. With a stable food supply, the world's population increased and communities grew larger. People had more time on their hands, so they turned to refining their skills at making tools and shelter and to developing writing, pottery, and other crafts.

Plants We Eat

This series examines the wide range of plants people around the world have chosen to eat. You will discover where plants came from, how they were first grown, how they traveled from their original homes, and where they have become important and why. Along the way, each book looks at the impact of certain plants on society and discusses the ways in which these food plants are sown, harvested, processed, and sold. You will also discover that some plants are key characters in exciting high-tech stories. And there are plenty of opportunities to test recipes and to dig into other hands-on activities.

The series Plants We Eat divides food plants into a variety of informal categories. Some plants are prized for their seeds, others for their fruits, and some for their underground roots, tubers, or bulbs. Many plants offer leaves or stalks for good eating. Humans convert some plants into oils and others into beverages or flavorings. In *Buried Treasure: Roots & Tubers*, we'll take a look at underground food treasures that come in the form of roots and tuberous swellings.

We don't know who first started poking around underground with a stick looking for edible roots and tubers. In loosening the soil, one of the earliest farming practices, this person was simply looking for something filling to eat. The part of a plant that grows up toward the sun is generally termed the stem. The part that pushes down into the ground is the root. The root brings water and minerals that are in the soil to the plant. Humans and livestock eat the roots of several plants, including cassava, carrots, turnips, beets, and radishes.

Some plants produce more food through photosynthesis than they can use. These plants store the extra nourishment in underground growths called tubers, which form at the tips of the roots. Tubers have small leaves and tiny buds that can develop into separate plants when divided from the parent plant and replanted. White and sweet potatoes and Jerusalem artichokes are perfect examples of true tuber-bearing plants. Other tuberous plants that are important regionally but are less well known throughout the world include yams, taro, and oca.

The word *tuber* comes from a Latin term meaning "swelling," so it's not surprising that people often call roots, tubers and tubers, roots—even though they are not quite the same thing. Take the cassava, for example. The roots of this tropical plant swell up with starchy food. Technically these swellings are not considered tubers, yet many people call the root of the cassava, after it's harvested, a tuber or a tuberous root.

Many roots and tubers grow wild and are rarely harvested on a large scale. *Buried Treasure: Roots & Tubers* examines white and sweet potatoes, cassava, carrots, turnips, beets, and radishes, all of which have been cultivated for thousands of years.

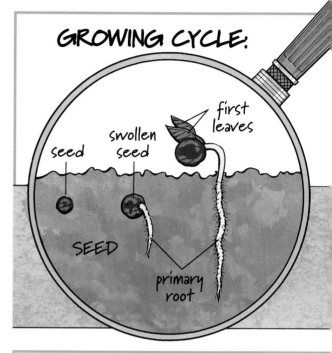

GROWING CYCLE:

seed
swollen seed
first leaves

SEED

primary root

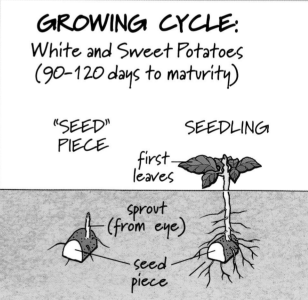

GROWING CYCLE:
White and Sweet Potatoes
(90–120 days to maturity)

"SEED" PIECE

SEEDLING

first leaves

sprout (from eye)

seed piece

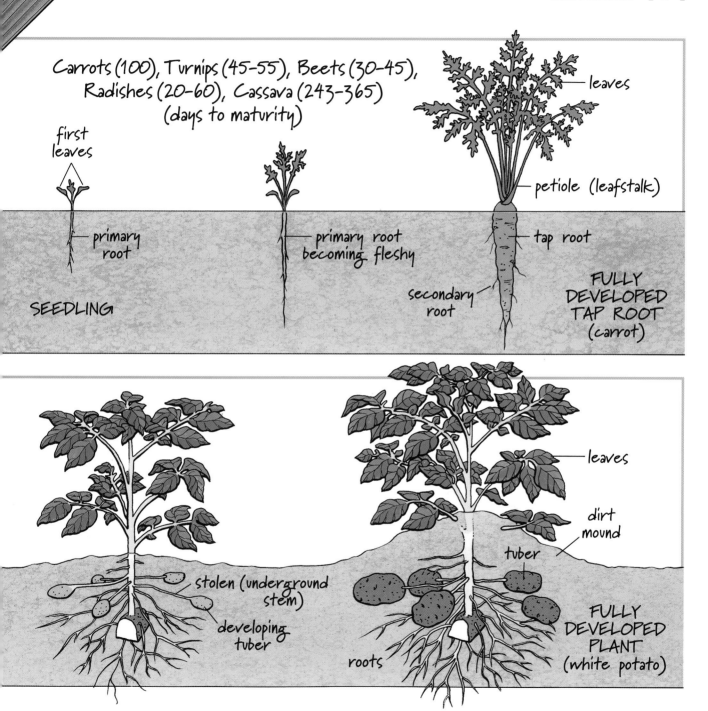

Carrots (100), Turnips (45-55), Beets (30-45),
Radishes (20-60), Cassava (243-365)
(days to maturity)

first leaves

primary root

SEEDLING

primary root becoming fleshy

leaves

petiole (leafstalk)

tap root

secondary root

FULLY DEVELOPED TAP ROOT (carrot)

stolen (underground stem)

developing tuber

leaves

dirt mound

tuber

roots

FULLY DEVELOPED PLANT (white potato)

Potatoes
[*Solanum tuberosum*]

One of the world's most important vegetables, the potato is closely related to many other edible plants, including eggplants, tomatoes, and peppers. Of this family, known as Solanaceae, only the eggplant hails from Asia. The rest of the family is from the Americas.

The potato first grew wild in the plateaus (elevated flatlands) of the Andes Mountains in western South America. Scientists known as paleobotanists have studied the middens, or trash heaps, of our human ancestors to learn more about the ancient origins of plants. Paleobotanists have found dried potato specimens dating back many thousands of years. From this discovery, the scientists concluded that people first cultivated potatoes in South America about 7,000 years ago.

Potatoes can yield a bumper (unusually large) crop! A farmer can harvest 40,000 pounds of potatoes from just one acre of land.

The man who has not anything to boast of but his illustrious ancestors is like a potato — the only good belonging to him is underground.

—Sir Thomas Overbury

Family Matters

To keep things straight in the huge families of plants and animals, scientists classify and name living things by grouping them according to shared features. These various characteristics become more noticeable in each of seven major categories. The categories are kingdom, division or phylum, class, order, family, genus, and species. Species share the most features in common, while members of a kingdom or division share far fewer traits. This system of scientific classification and naming is called taxonomy. Scientists refer to plants and animals by a two-part Latin or Greek term made up of the genus and the species name. The genus name comes first, followed by the species name. Look at the potato's taxonomic name on page 10. Can you figure out to what genus the potato belongs? And to what species?

Early History

The earliest settlers of the harsh, cool Andean highlands chose the area in large part because the wild potato grew there. Abundant, nourishing food makes even the toughest landscape attractive to people. Early gatherers soon learned which plant species tasted best and which kept longest after they were picked.

The plant itself taught the region's first farmers that to get a potato, you plant a potato. Early Andean peoples tossed their potato peels and excess tubers into garbage heaps.

The soils that cover the towering Andes of South America gave birth to the potato.

An engraving shows people harvesting potatoes in Peru, one of the Andean nations of South America.

The discarded tubers took hold and grew into new plants. Eventually someone discovered the tubers of the new plants and dug them up. Imitating what they had seen with the garbage pile, the earliest farmers may have placed potatoes on the ground and thrown some soil on top. Or they may have dug holes into the earth, thinking that where the tuber first came from might also be a good place to plant it. By trying different ways of growing things, people came to know what method worked best.

The earliest potato farmers of the Andes relied on tools similar to those still in use in the region. Farmers maneuvered tall foot plows to break open the soil for planting in the spring. After the plant foliage had died back in the summer, small hand tools easily dug up the mounds of potatoes lying hidden just underground.

Farming supplied Andean peoples such as the Incas with a stable food supply. By the 1400s, the cultivation of the potato had enabled the Incas to establish a vast and populous empire along the western coast of South America. The potato—one of the Incas' main food crops—was also an important trade item. Inca traders from highland areas exchanged potatoes for maize (corn) grown by farmers in the coastal parts of the empire.

Small military units sent out from the Incan capital of Cuzco (in modern-day Peru) to patrol the empire survived on portions of *chuño*—freeze-dried, dehydrated potatoes. Grated for bread or popped into a pot of boiling broth for stew, chuño was the world's first fast food.

In search of gold, silver, and other treasures, well-armed Spanish conquistadores (conquerors) arrived in Inca lands in the 1500s. By 1532 the Spanish had destroyed the unity of the empire and largely enslaved its people. By seizing the Incas' potato warehouses and other food stores, the conquerors dominated daily life. They forced the Incas to work long hours in the area's gold and silver mines and almost succeeded in eliminating Incan culture.

From the Andes, the Spanish brought the potato to Europe. The potato's first voyage eastward across the Atlantic Ocean was not recorded, but a cook probably tossed some potatoes into a ship's stores to feed the crew during the trip back to Spain. Somehow a few tubers made it off the ship and into a Spanish garden or two. Patients at a hospital in Seville, Spain, were

Pronunciation = CHOO-nyoh

It's a Fact!

Who do you suppose first figured out that it's safe to eat the underground tubers of the potato plant but not its small, green, tomato-like fruits? These small fruits (which rarely form in modern commercial varieties) as well as the plant's leaves and stalks are highly toxic. A few folks probably suffered terrible stomachaches and died while gaining this knowledge.

probably the first to sample the potato. The purchase of potatoes as food for the hospital was duly noted in the hospital's records in 1573.

The Well-Traveled Potato

How did a tiny tuber from the Andes Mountains become one of the world's most important vegetables? By fits and starts. Carried by Roman Catholic monks from Spain, the potato was initially planted in monastery gardens of southern Europe. By the early 1600s, traveling church officials and explorers returning from South America had helped the potato make its way throughout northern Europe and what became the British Isles.

To reach North America, the potato traveled back across the Atlantic Ocean from the British Isles and quietly took root wherever British colonists settled. Captain John Smith—one of the founders of Jamestown, Virginia, the first permanent English settlement in North America—is said to have noted potatoes planted in Virginia about 1620. In 1685 William Penn, the founder of Pennsylvania, observed potatoes growing in gardens there. By 1719 the first intensive commercial cultivation of potatoes was under way in New Hampshire with the arrival of Scotch-Irish settlers.

Meanwhile, potato pioneers were popping up in every country in Europe, despite the fact that even into the 1700s many people still viewed the potato with suspicion. Underground vegetables have often been cast as the bad guys. It didn't help that potatoes belong to the Solanaceae (nightshade) family, which includes several plants that Europeans knew to be poisonous. Many people were simply afraid to eat the potato. A

The settlement at Jamestown, Virginia, endured severe hardships until the residents successfully grew their own food, including potatoes.

few towns in Europe even banned growing potatoes for fear that eating the tuber caused disease. In addition, some Europeans wouldn't taste foods that hadn't been written about in the Bible.

Other people, however, recognized the power of the potato. During the late 1700s, Benjamin Thompson, Count von Rumford, organized soup kitchens for the poor of Bavaria (a state in present-day Germany) and served up rich stews made mainly of potatoes. The hungry recipients thought they were eating turnips, a more familiar vegetable of the era. At about the same time, a pharmacist named Antoine-Auguste Parmentier was devoting himself to pushing the potato in his native France. As a prisoner of war during the Seven Years' War (1756–1763), Parmentier had been fed the tuber by his German captors, who viewed the potato as fit only for pigs. Back in France, Parmentier convinced King Louis XVI to let him plant a garden of potatoes outside Paris. Heavily guarded by day, the garden attracted locals, who came at night to steal the plants for their own plots.

The potato took a while to catch on in some parts of Europe. One of its cheerleaders was Benjamin Thompson *(below)*, a British scientist and politician who worked for the king of Bavaria. Another potato supporter was Antoine-Auguste Parmentier *(below left, kneeling)*, who introduced the tuber to France. Here, he hands King Louis XVI one of the fruits of his labors.

This plant is suffering from late blight, the fungal disease that destroyed Ireland's potato crop in the mid-1800s.

Part of the Spanish Armada that tried and failed to invade England

Parmentier may have succeeded almost too well. Soon royals were wearing potato flowers in their hats, and fabric and pottery makers were designing floral patterns based on the potato flower. When Parmentier was about to be nominated for a city job, one of the voters declared, "He will make us eat nothing but potatoes, he it is who invented them!"

Ireland, the Potato's Second Home

Nowhere except in the Andes Mountains of South America has the potato seemed more at home than in Ireland. Its arrival there is unclear. Some accounts claim that Spanish battleships ran aground on the Irish coast during a sea battle with England in 1588. The ship's supply of potatoes washed ashore, where the locals grabbed them up.

By the 1700s, the English, long at odds with the Irish, ruled Ireland. The Irish—who had previously relied almost exclusively on oats and milk for their everyday food—were eating 8 to 12 pounds of potatoes apiece each day. Irish farmers lived on land owned by the English. The Irish grew wheat and other grains on the land as payment of rent to the English landowners. Irish families were able to survive by planting potatoes on whatever small plots remained. Because Ireland's many poor families thus depended totally on the potato, the stage was set for disaster.

The disaster came in the form of a moisture-loving fungus called *Phytophthora infestans,* or late blight, a disease that blackens the plant's leaves before moving down the stem to rot the underground tubers. Even harvested and stored potatoes can carry the fungus and be wiped out.

After the blight hit Ireland, hundreds of thousands left the country. Here, relatives in County Kerry say their final good-byes before heading for America.

Imagine having only one primary food, one vegetable to eat every day, year in, year out. And then consider having that food source destroyed within weeks. When the blight hit Irish fields in 1845, it obliterated every potato in the ground, every tuber stored in every corner of every cottage. Ordinary Irish people, who depended on the potato for their food and for their means to barter for other items, were destitute. Unable to pay the rent to their British landlords, thousands and thousands were evicted from their homes. Roving groups of men, women, and children huddled by the roadsides eating grass in front of wispy fires. Those who did not die from starvation fell victim to diseases such as typhus, dysentery, and scurvy.

The Great Famine, also known as the Great Hunger, changed Ireland forever. While some landlords aided their tenants by reducing rents and distributing grains, many others did nothing. British relief efforts were poorly organized and came too late. At least 1 million people died, and more than 1.5 million left Ireland for North America and Australia. The population of Ireland fell from nearly 9 million to about 4 million in just a few years.

A Japanese woodblock print of Matthew Perry

The Potato Goes To Asia

Written records of the potato's appearance are few, but food historians know that the potato arrived in China and Japan during the 1600s. For years the Japanese enjoyed the potato plant solely for its delicate flowers. In 1853 U.S. naval officer Matthew Perry visited Japan. Perry arrived with warships bristling with guns and a wide array of gifts, including a barrel of potatoes. His mission was to open Japanese ports to trade after long years of isolation. The emperor of Japan evidently ate some potatoes and seemed satisfied. From then on, potatoes appeared on Japanese dinner tables.

In the Japanese city of Hokkaido, a vendor offers roasted potatoes for sale.

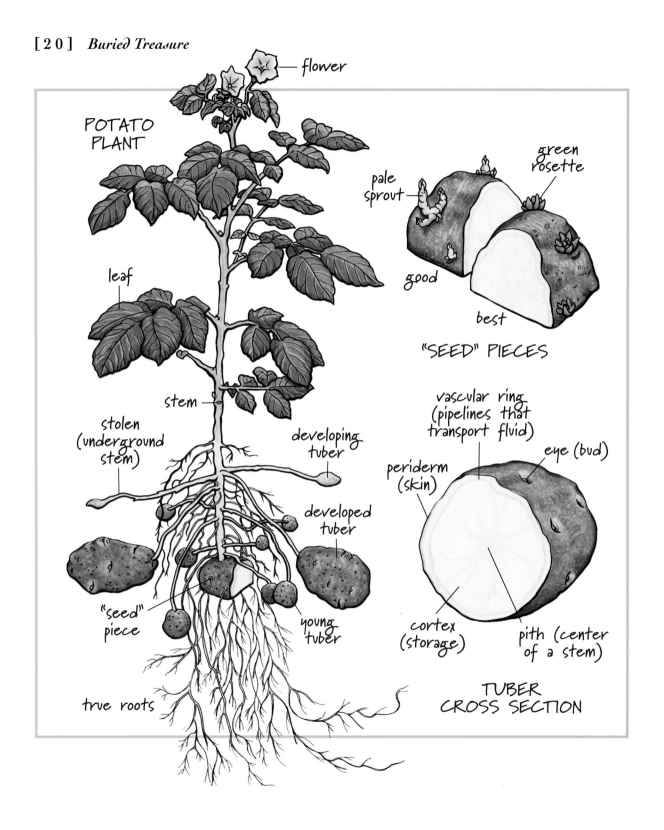

POTATO PLANT

flower

leaf

stem

stolen (underground stem)

developing tuber

developed tuber

"seed" piece

young tuber

true roots

pale sprout

green rosette

good

best

"SEED" PIECES

vascular ring (pipelines that transport fluid)

periderm (skin)

eye (bud)

cortex (storage)

pith (center of a stem)

TUBER CROSS SECTION

While potatoes are growing underground, the plants develop flowers that vary from white to shades of pink and purple.

Planting, Digging, and Storing Potatoes

Farmers in more than 75 percent of the world's countries—from the frigid lands of the Arctic to the deserts of Israel—grow potatoes. Farmers in all of the 50 United States raise the tuber, with Idaho, Washington, and Colorado topping the list. China produces the most potatoes in the world, many to be traded for rice, but most to feed livestock. Russia leads Europe in potato production. The Netherlands is the world's leading exporter of seed potatoes, small tubers grown solely for planting. The Netherlands also grows acres of table potatoes and produces the bulk of the world's potato starch for use in manufacturing and in high technology.

It's a Fact!

Potatoes are often called "spuds," a term that comes from an old English word meaning "dagger" and that refers to a spadelike tool for digging or cutting. Before mechanized farming, people planted and harvested potatoes with spuds.

All over the world, farmers plant seed potatoes when the plants' **eyes** (buds) sprout. In fact, you can even grow a potato at home from a small piece of potato skin, as long as that skin has an eye. From a single potato or piece of potato grows a tall plant with many tubers swelling underground.

The San Luis Valley in southern Colorado is a perfect potato home. Lying at about 8,000 feet above sea level between the Sangre de Cristo and the San Juan Mountains, the area produces superb potatoes each fall, most sold as fresh table potatoes. Underground aquifers (naturally occurring storehouses of water) provide farmers with water to irrigate row after row of potato plants in this semiarid (dry) landscape. Here, as throughout the world, commercial potato farmers rely on high-speed machines to plant their crops. The machines span six rows at a time. They plow up a row, drop in the seed potatoes and fertilizers, and cover them with a mound of soil, all in swift repetitive motion. If the tubers are exposed to sun, they turn green and become bitter. The green comes from the pigment chlorophyll and indicates the presence of the poison solanine. To protect the tubers from the sun, tractors come through the rows periodically to mound up the earth at the base of the plants as they grow.

Planting time differs depending on geographic location. Potatoes are sensitive to sunburn and frost. Farmers in hot southern areas of the United States, for example, plant from September through March when the heat of the sun is less intense. Northern planters, on the other hand, usually have to wait until late spring or early summer to avoid damaging frosts.

With the help of a seed tractor *(left)*, workers are able to plant several rows of potatoes at the same time. *(Facing page, left)* Tractors build hills of soil to protect the young underground plants from sunlight.

Many farmers rely on toxic chemicals to control the diseases and insects that attack potato plants. Insecticides, for example, fight off potato beetles, potato tuber worms, and other insects that attack potato plants. These chemicals are either sprayed into the soil at planting time or are applied to the growing plants. Farmers spray potato plants with fungicides to control damaging funguses and other plant diseases.

After only 90 to 120 days—faster than most any other **staple crop**—the potatoes are ready to harvest. Farmers drive machines called diggers or harvesters into the fields. The machines remove the surface leaves and stalks, dig up the potatoes, and pull them up a conveyor belt into a large bin. As the potatoes rattle along the belt, rocks and pebbles drop through a grid onto the ground, and the vines are tossed out the back of the harvester. Trucks follow alongside the huge machines, taking mounds of potatoes directly to the storage areas where the spuds are sorted to size and then bagged.

(Top) Farmers spray their fields with chemicals to destroy pests such as the Colorado potato beetle (inset). (Above) After the above-ground potato plants have died off, it's time to harvest. Workers on large farms dig up potatoes with a mechanical harvester.

In sharp contrast to these methods, many Andean peoples still plant and harvest potatoes as their ancestors did. Using tall foot plows of curved wood and forged metal, they cultivate steep slopes where mechanized vehicles would be unsuitable.

The Quechua Indians of Peru, for example, live in the clear mountain air of the Andes at about 12,000 feet above sea level. Here, growing potatoes is a family affair—the man plows up the soil, and the woman loosens the clumps of soil with a hoe. She then drops the potatoes by hand from a sack and treads them into the dirt with her foot. The Quechua grow hundreds of different varieties of potatoes, knowing exactly which strain is best suited to each type of soil, terrain, and temperature.

At harvesttime entire families work the fields. Women and children often build an oven from dirt clods right in the row. Potatoes for lunch or dinner can then be baked on the spot, fired by the dried stalks and leaves of the potato plant itself.

Storage of fresh potatoes for eating, whether dug by machine or by hand, has

(*Right*) On smaller farms, harvesting is done by hand. Here, a Peruvian woman shows off her crop. (*Facing page*) Farmers in the Asian nation of Nepal store their harvested potatoes in a deep pit.

long been a dilemma. Folks around the world have resolved the problem in different ways. Potatoes can't be too hot or they'll sprout. They can't be left out in the sunlight or they'll turn green. Potatoes can't be allowed to freeze or they'll discolor and become too sugary. Potatoes like consistent, cool but not freezing temperatures and steady levels of humidity. They store well in cellars and in well-covered mounds called clamps. Large-scale producers of potatoes house their harvests in spacious storage buildings where temperature and humidity can be carefully controlled to provide consumers with potatoes year-round. Small-scale farmers in less developed areas of the world such as Nepal store potatoes in underground pits, digging up the tubers as needed.

Dig In!

To plant a potato, buy a small, specially grown seed potato from a garden center. Set the seed potato to sprout on a windowsill that doesn't get direct sunlight. The sprouting takes a few days. Then find a flowerpot that's about eight inches in diameter. Fill it two-thirds full of potting soil, set the seed potato in place with the sprout end up, cover it with soil, and water well. Set the potted potato in a sunny spot in your home.

Water the potato periodically to keep it moist but not soaked. After several days, when leaves show, add more loose soil to make a mound at the base of the plant. (Remember, tubers become bitter if exposed to sunlight.) Continue mounding up the soil and watering the potato as the plant grows, until there's no more room in the pot. When the foliage turns brown and withers, it's time to start digging for buried treasure.

To Your Health!

Take a potato and cut it in half. What do you see inside? Moisture. Potatoes are 75 percent water, very similar to your own body, believe it or not. See anything else? What you can't see in a potato is its power. Potatoes are loaded with starch carbohydrates, which give endurance athletes the energy to keep moving over the long haul. Potatoes are a good source of protein, of vitamin C, and of B vitamins.

And, with no oil or fat and very little sodium, potatoes are a healthy, low-fat, energy-filled food. Until you drop it in a vat of fat. To eat well and stay healthy, eat potatoes boiled, mashed, or baked instead—and without butter and sour cream. Try salsa or low-fat cottage cheese for a change.

New technology, however, may save the day for fried-potato lovers. Researchers are finding that absorption of fats from cooking oil is reduced by 60 percent if French fries are coated—before frying—with a thin layer of potato starch.

We Are All Potato Eaters

People like to eat potatoes or the plant would not have taken hold in so many places, so far from the plant's South American origins. The people of the mountainous regions of China, Peru, Bolivia, Tibet, Ecuador, Rwanda, and Nepal eat potatoes daily as their staple food, topping them with assorted spices and sauces. In parts of Southeast Asia, potatoes are considered luxury foods. On the island of Luzon in the Philippines, potatoes are individually washed and wrapped in plastic, ready for sale in the market. Belgium lays claim to originating *frites* (French fries). In

World War I (1914–1918), U.S. soldiers stationed in the southern, French-speaking part of Belgium feasted on fried potatoes that they dubbed "Frenchy fries." Ever since then, English speakers have given France the credit for a worldwide favorite.

New Potato Uses

The potato fascinates scientists all over the world. Peru, for instance, is the home of the International Potato Center, where scientists from around the globe research the potato, developing new varieties and better ways to grow potatoes in varying climates and soils. Remember the Irish potato blight? Mexico is the center for scientific work on late blight, the disease that caused the Irish potato famine and still attacks potato plants. Scientists have found wild, blight-resistant potatoes in Mexico and are developing domesticated potatoes that will have a natural immunity to the fungus. Fighting plant enemies this way will help farmers avoid resorting to expensive and toxic chemical sprays.

Dutch industrial potatoes dominate the high-tech world of starch products. Sticky, white, and slightly sweet, potato starch makes up the bulk of the potato's dry matter and is widely used in a vast array of everyday products. Paper is coated with it for strength. Starch helps lipsticks and many other cosmetics hold together and is an ingredient in glues and medicine capsules. More and more prepared foods—such as instant soups, baked goods, and microwave dinners—are made from potato starch, too. Potato starch is a substitute for fat in a range of nonfat or low-fat food products and is even a player in the high-tech arena of medicine.

A woman from Estonia, a country in eastern Europe, digs up potatoes from a field near her home.

For global potato information: International Potato Center in Lima, Peru, at www.cgiar.org/CIP/ciphome.htm

Biodegradable plastics are another star potato product. For example, people in the Netherlands use degradable plastic bags made from potato starch to store their household waste. Athletes at the 1994 Winter Olympic Games in Lillehammer, Norway, ate their cafeteria meals on small trays made almost entirely of potato starch by a company in Sweden. When the meals were over, cleanup staff simply tossed the trays into compost piles, where the trays disintegrated within six to nine months. Some daring athletes, learning their plates were made from

These thriving potato plants got their start in a nutrient-rich solution that NASA scientists are testing for use on future space stations.

potatoes, more than licked their platters clean. They ate them!

A potato-derived fuel called ethanol is well known in potato-growing areas of the world. Germans have used potato ethanol to power vehicles, to illuminate streetlights, and to fire up stoves. North American potato farmers often run farm vehicles on fuel made from extra potatoes, saving fuel costs and making use of a renewable source of energy.

Are you getting the idea that the potato is an international pioneer? It's more than that—its extraterrestrial. In 1996 the potato kicked off the science of astroculture to become the first food grown in space. Carried aloft on the space shuttle *Columbia*, the bud-carrying cuttings from the Norland variety of potatoes grew in a small, boxy, growing chamber designed by scientists at the University of Wisconsin. Nurtured on nutrients mixed in a water solution, the cuttings did indeed produce tiny red-skinned tubers during their two-week space voyage.

It's likely that space stations will eventually grow a range of foods for use by travelers moving out into the stars. Scientists chose the potato because it produces food efficiently in severely restricted growing spaces and provides more protein and slow-release energy than any other food tested. Potatoes also leave little waste, are easily cooked, and just as importantly, most people like to eat them.

Dig In!

LEFTOVER MASHIEBURGERS
(4—6 servings)

2 cups leftover mashed potatoes
¼ cup flour
1 egg
salt and pepper, to taste
a pinch of oregano or tarragon

Mix the mashed potatoes with your choice of chopped vegetables, nuts, or cheese from the list. Use your imagination. Try just cheese, or cheese plus red pepper, or beans and nuts—whatever combination appeals to you.

Add the egg, flour, salt and pepper, and herbs. Mix well. Form burger-shaped patties of the mashie mix. Lightly coat a skillet with olive oil and cook the patties on medium until golden brown. Turn only once. Serve piping hot with horseradish sauce, hot sauce, ketchup, curry sauce, or sour cream—or none of the above.

¼ cup each of any combination of the following—
    grated cheese, finely chopped green onions, grated carrots, diced red pepper, chopped mushrooms, finely chopped zucchini, ground walnuts, or chopped, cooked green beans

The recipe for leftover mashieburgers gives the cook plenty of freedom. Because the recipe deals with leftovers, amounts are somewhat loose.

Sweet Potatoes
[*Ipomoea batatas*]

Despite the similarity of their names, the potato and the sweet potato are not at all related. In fact, botanists (plant scientists) still argue about whether the sweet potato is officially a tuber or a root. We're going with tuber. The sweet potato is the only member of the large Convolvulaceae family that humans eat. The sweet potato's close cousin, the morning glory, is a favorite of many home gardeners, who love this vining plant and its colorful blue, pink, or white flowers.

Christopher Columbus never saw a potato, but then he never explored the mountainous western coast of South America. Early in his explorations of the islands in the Caribbean Sea, however, Columbus dined on several different varieties of sweet potato. Sweet potatoes thrived in the area's warm, tropical climate and were a common food in the regional diet. In his diary, Columbus compared the sweet potato to a large radish

Sweet potatoes *(right)* and yams sometimes look very similar, but they are not the same. Sweets are from the plant family Convolvulaceae and thrive in several U.S. states, while yams, which are not grown in the United States, belong to the Dioscoreaceae family.

Let the sky rain [sweet] potatoes!

—Falstaff

(Above) During his travels to lands in the Caribbean Sea, Christopher Columbus dined on sweet potatoes and introduced them to Spain. (Facing page) Sweet potatoes dominate a market in Papua New Guinea.

in size and to a roasted chestnut in taste. Columbus later presented the sweet potato to his patrons, King Ferdinand and Queen Isabella of Spain.

Some food historians believe that native peoples may have been cultivating sweet potatoes in the islands of the mid-Pacific Ocean and in New Zealand long before Columbus discovered the tubers in the Americas. One theory is that South Americans may have carried the plant across the Pacific Ocean to the islands of Polynesia. Another theory is that the ocean-going Polynesians sailed far beyond their home islands to the coast of South America, returning home with the sweet-tasting new tuber. Polynesians may even have carried the sweet potato to Southeast Asia and from there to the African continent.

Spanish expeditions in the early 1500s to what would become Mexico and Brazil found local peoples eating sweet potatoes there. The Spanish brought the potatoes to Europe, where people liked the sweet tuber because of its high sugar content. Some Europeans even considered the plant to be an aphrodisiac, or a love potion. Because the sweet potato was not well suited for growing in Europe's rainy, cool climate, it had to be imported from Spain's colonies in the faraway Americas. Only wealthy Europeans could afford to pay the high price for the tubers.

The British explorer Captain James Cook encountered sweet potatoes for the first time when he visited the Hawaiian Islands in 1778. He received the sweets as a gift from the local sailors who paddled out to greet his ship. A later visitor to Hawaii, U.S. naval explorer Charles Wilkes, described seeing 33 varieties of sweet potato under cultivation in 1845.

Sweet Potatoes in Papua New Guinea

The introduction of a plant to a new place may become successful in ways people cannot anticipate. Anthropologist John Reader contends that such was true in Papua New Guinea, a group of islands in the western Pacific Ocean, where the sweet potato arrived in the 1600s. The easy cultivation and growth of the sweet potato meant each family had more surplus food to feed to their pigs, the primary source of animal protein. Before they had sweet potatoes, communities held feasts at harvesttime. Pigs fattened on garden surplus were killed and shared among families and neighbors at the feasts.

A Tale of Two Tubers

Taino-speaking peoples of the Caribbean region called sweet potatoes *batatas*. In Spain the tubers became known as *patatas*. When the sweets made it to England, people there called them "potatoes." When potatoes later arrived in Europe, folks assumed that potatoes and sweet potatoes were related and called them by the same name. Although the two tubers are not botanically related, the name has stuck for both food plants.

Over time, however, the pigs became symbols of wealth and power. Instead of feeding the pigs only the excess from the garden, families allowed their gardens to become the pig's pantry. With large crops of sweet potatoes, families raised more pigs. And more pigs meant more wealth and status for a few male elders.

The community's diet changed. Instead of eating only a few pigs on a fairly regular basis, people slaughtered thousands at gift-giving festivals called *moka*. At the festivals, people gorged on pork, some even dying of overconsumption. After the moka celebration, the cycle began again—the intense cultivation of sweet potatoes to the exclusion of other foods, the slow accumulation of pigs, and so on. The result? A decline in the health of the island peoples and an increased burden on the farmers of the area, mostly women, to produce food for pigs rather than for people.

Famine Food for Japan

On the other hand, the sweet potato saved people in both Japan and China from starvation more than once. Smuggled out of the Spanish-controlled Philippines and into China as early as 1594, the tuber rescued the southern Chinese from famine due to failure of the rice crop. Brought to the Japanese island of Okinawa in 1605, the sweet potato was prized by locals for its durability. The hardy tuber resisted insect attacks and survived the seasonal typhoons (windy, tropical storms) that devastated rice plantations. With the sweet potato, people could still be well fed even if the rice crops failed.

In the mid-1700s, a shogun (Japanese military governor) who was impressed by the plant's food value and ease of cultivation became determined to spread its use throughout Japan. He turned to an unlikely but ultimately successful promoter—Konyo Aoki, a government official and scholar of Confucianism (an ancient philosophy originally developed in China). Aoki wrote and distributed a book of instructions to farmers in the greater Tokyo area. The book detailed how to grow and store sweet potatoes and even included seed potatoes for the farmers to plant.

Over the years, the sweet potato in Japan stepped in when other crops failed and proved resilient even during war. In 1945, at the end of World War II, the

It's a Fact!

During Tokyo's annual sweet potato festival, people visit the grave of Konyo Aoki, the scholar credited with starting sweet potato cultivation in the Tokyo area in the 1700s.

The sweet potato is popular in other parts of Asia, too. In Vietnam farmers set the tuber in the sun to dry.

United States dropped atomic bombs to destroy the Japanese cities of Hiroshima and Nagasaki. Many citizens of Hiroshima survived the devastation of the atomic blast by living on nutritious sweet potatoes. The tubers, growing safely under the soil, remained uncontaminated by the effects of nuclear fallout (toxic radioactive debris) from the bomb. After the war, rural Japanese faced with food shortages lived on *suiton,* a dish of chopped sweet potato leaves and vines mixed with rice.

In modern high-tech Japanese society, the sweet potato has a firm foothold. In winter vendors of *yaki-imo,* or grilled sweet potatoes, push their carts through town, roasting sweet potatoes over small wood fires.

In some parts of Indonesia, people steam their food over an open fire on a bed of sweet potato leaves and vines.

The blooms of the sweet potato plant look a bit like those of their cousins, the morning glory.

Japanese cities feature shops that sell pastries, ice cream, and custard desserts—all made from sweet potatoes. Deep-fried sweet potato hunks slathered with a sticky syrup constitute "university potatoes," a dish designed for the sweetest of sweet tooths, most of them, presumably, the property of students.

But the vegetable is not just sweet. The Japanese cultivate dozens of sweet potato varieties, many of them with dry textures and barely any sugar. In Kawagoe, Japan, you can dine on a seven-course meal in a fine restaurant dedicated to presenting cuisine based solely on the sweet potato. Noodles with sophisticated sauces, battered and deep-fried tempura, aromatic soups, and subtle desserts are all made from the tubers of one remarkable plant.

Vietnam Farmer Locks Himself Up With Giant Potato

HANOI, VIETNAM. A farmer in central Vietnam has locked himself in his house with a giant sweet potato, the Lao Dong daily said on Thursday. Weighing in at [187 pounds] the sweet potato was discovered by Vo Nhu Da last Saturday. But word of his find spread fast and before long he was inundated with throngs of curious visitors.

"Hearing about the strange sweet potato, people came thousands of times to Da's house for a look, and so he had to take it into a room and lock the door," the paper said.

(Reuters, February 1, 1996)

The North American Sweet

The sweet potato came to the United States with European colonists. Raised in Virginia as early as 1610, sweet potatoes eventually were raised on large plantations in the Carolinas. Plantation slaves from Africa grew the sweets alongside their cabins, close to the cooking pot. They probably began the custom of calling the potatoes yams, since the tubers resembled a similar tropical plant the slaves knew from their home continent.

After the U.S. Civil War, which took place between the Northern and the Southern states from 1861 until 1865, poor Southern farmers relied on sweet potatoes to improve their poor-quality soils. The farmers would allow sweet potato vines to decay on the ground and then work them into the ground as a natural fertilizer. They even used the vines to feed their livestock in times of drought, when pastures were scorched by the hot sun and lack of rain.

This photograph from 1862 shows a group of slaves planting sweet potatoes on a plantation in South Carolina.

Growing and Curing Sweets

Farmers around the world grow sweet potatoes. China harvests about 85 percent of the world's sweet potatoes. In the United States, North Carolina, Louisiana, and California are the nation's top producers of the tubers.

Sweet potatoes develop from slips, or small growths put out by the plant's roots. Farmers place seed sweet potatoes in moist, sandy planting beds that are warmed to 75° F or 80° F to ensure sprouting. After the sprouts reach 8 to 10 inches in length, the slips are cut off from the root and are planted about 12 inches apart in rows spaced approx-

A farmer in Japan, where sweet potatoes are hugely popular, uses a hand-guided machine to harvest his crop.

imately three feet apart. North American farmers usually plant with machines called transplanters, which can span four rows. But people are still needed to actually place the slips in the ground. They select slips from boxed bundles, dropping the plants into the rows. As the machine moves ahead, it releases a precise amount of water onto the plant as the soil is pulled around it.

After about 90 days, the tubers are ready for harvest. First the extensive network of sweet potato vines must be cut because they are easily entangled with the equipment that unearths the potatoes. A variety of machines, some modified from those that harvest white potatoes, uncover the sweet potatoes. Some of the machines can handle both cutting the vines and digging up the tubers.

No matter what equipment a farmer uses, some bruising of the tubers does occur. This is why sweet potatoes must be cured (dried). After they're packed in field boxes, the sweet potatoes are transported to storage facilities where the tubers remain in curing areas for about five days. The high humidity and high temperature of the curing stage help to heal any superficial wounds the potatoes may have received in handling. Curing also aids in preventing diseases from attacking the plants. After the curing phase, the temperature in storage is lowered from 80° F to about 60° F. The tubers are then washed and sorted before shipment to market.

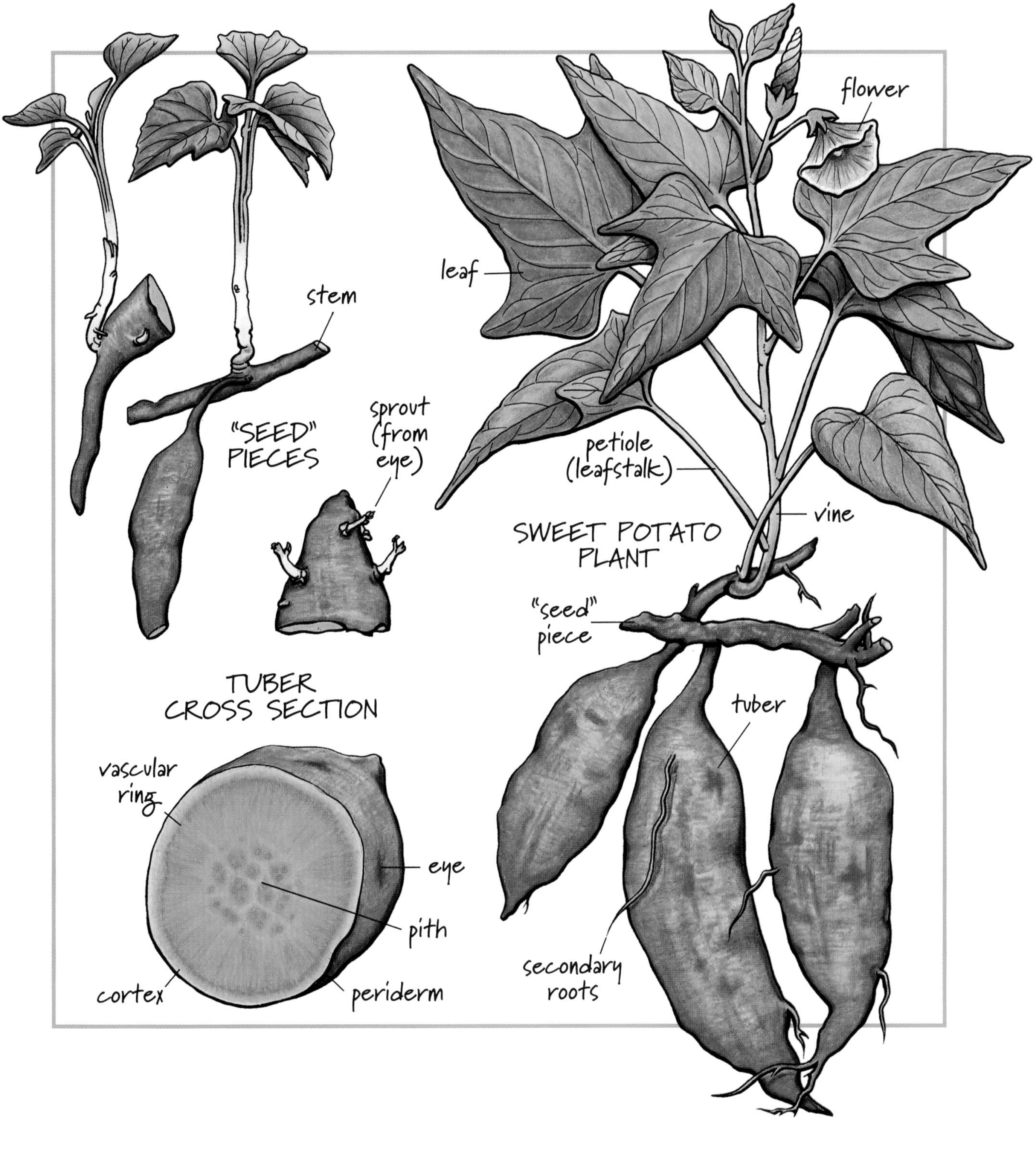

"SEED" PIECES

stem

sprout (from eye)

SWEET POTATO PLANT

leaf

flower

petiole (leafstalk)

vine

"seed" piece

tuber

secondary roots

TUBER CROSS SECTION

vascular ring

eye

pith

cortex

periderm

In China farmers frequently **intercrop** (mix) sweet potato plants with other crops to make the best use of water and to promote greater resistance to insects. A typical grouping in Szechwan, China, features a row of mulberry trees with a small plot of sweet potatoes, rice plants, and Chinese cabbage under the trees. All these crops are planted and fertilized by hand. At harvesttime farm workers dig up the sweets with hand tools and toss them into long, woven baskets on their backs.

Sweet Potatoes around the World

Sweet potatoes have never caught on in the United States or Canada as a true food staple. Sweets are usually available to the general public in just one or two sugary-tasting varieties. Some grocers even view these

A woman in Indonesia washes and cleans sweet potatoes near a river.

To Your Health!

You'll see like a cat at night with vitamin A! Sweet potatoes are packed with beta-carotene, which the body converts into vitamin A. Vitamin A is important in maintaining eyesight (especially night vision) and in preserving healthy skin and teeth. The vitamin also helps repair damaged body tissues and protects them from infection.

Farmers in North Carolina *(left)* lead the United States in commercial sweet potato production, with their closest competitors being growers in Louisiana and California.

as poor keepers, because the tubers tend to bruise and spoil easily. The plant is still a significant commercial crop in the southern United States, however, and is shipped to markets across the nation.

Some North Americans do enjoy eating the sweet potato, of course. What was once just an ingredient in sweet potato casserole slathered with marshmallows, a common Thanksgiving dish, is also used in pies, puddings, smooth tangy soups, stir-fried dishes, as well as by itself, just baked. With large Korean and Japanese populations in California, local sweet potato growers are beginning to plant Japanese varieties, many of which taste like a mild squash.

These same growers ship some of their sweets east to Florida to meet the demand of that state's growing West Indian population, who use sweet potatoes on a regular basis. Jamaicans, for example, eat a sweet pudding called pone made from sweet potatoes and ginger. Ginger wine is an ingredient in a Cuban dish that calls for mashed sweet potatoes as a main ingredient in this light, egg-filled cake.

Dig In!

GLAZED SWEET POTATOES (4 servings)

2 tablespoons butter
1 teaspoon sugar or honey
1 tablespoon raisins
a pinch of salt
½ teaspoon ground ginger
1 teaspoon cinnamon
juice of one lemon

grated rind of one orange
2 tablespoons water
2 sweet potatoes, sliced and boiled on top of the stove for two or three minutes or microwaved for a couple of minutes to slightly soften the slices but not cook them through

Melt the butter in a heavy skillet over medium heat. Mix in the sugar or honey and the raisins. Next add the salt, ginger, cinnamon, lemon juice, and orange rind. Mix well before adding the water. Add the partially cooked potato slices, stirring to coat them with the sauce. Cover the pan and cook the potatoes on low heat for 5 to 10 minutes, turning them from time to time so they cook evenly.

Glazed sweet potatoes are a South African side dish.

Sweet Potatoes Go High-Tech

George Washington Carver, the tireless plant scientist, worked at Tuskegee Institute in Tuskegee, Alabama, during the first half of the 1900s. He focused his studies on the sweet potato's potential as a source of manufactured products. Carver saw more in the plant than just good eating. From it he made 118 products, including alcohol, shoe polish, postage stamp glue, bluing liquid (a bleaching agent), rubber, and color washes.

Carver would have welcomed the role of the sweet potato in the modern-day production of ethanol, an alternative to gasoline. Indonesia has replaced sugarcane with sweet potatoes as the basis of its ethanol program. The sweet potato produces five times the fuel of sugarcane and can be harvested more frequently throughout the year.

(Left) The International Institute of Tropical Agriculture (IITA), which is headquartered in Nigeria, is developing new sweet potato varieties. *(Above)* Born into slavery, the U.S. botanist George Washington Carver won his freedom when slavery was abolished in 1865. He tirelessly pursued formal education, receiving a bachelor's and a master's degree in agriculture. Carver devoted his life not only to developing better agricultural methods but also to improving relations among various U.S. ethnic groups.

Cassava

[*Manihot esculenta*]

Preparing a little cassava for dinner happens every day throughout a huge part of the world. Native to the tropical regions of Mexico, Central America, and South America, cassava is known by many names—manioc, *mandioca*, *manioca*, tapioca, Brazilian arrowroot, and yuca. The Tupí-Guaraní Indians of the Amazon region in South America were growing this root plant about 5,000 years ago in areas of present-day Colombia and Venezuela. The two varieties of cassava—bitter and sweet—both contain a toxin called hydrocyanic or prussic acid. Both types of cassava require special handling to remove the toxin before eating. The native peoples who grew up with the plant could tell the bitter from the sweet just by looking at it.

Fresh cassava are for sale at a market on the East African island of Zanzibar.

Salt they never use in it [cassava bread], which I wonder at; for the bread being tasteless of it selfe, they should give it some little seasoning.

—Richard Ligon

The Maya, for example, early inhabitants of the Yucatán area of Mexico, regularly ate roasted manioc (the sweet kind). The Aztecs, a later group from Mexico's central plains, had access only to the bitter cassava, so they ate it less often.

Cassava in Motion

Christopher Columbus, the first European to taste many American foods, wrote feverishly about everything he ate during his travels. In 1492 Arawak

It's a Fact!

The word *cassava* may have its origin in Taíno, the language of the Arawak Indians. The Arawaks called their cassava bread *casabe* or *cazabe*, which the Spanish most likely mispronounced as "cassava." The word *tapioca* comes from the Tupí-Guaraní Indians of the Amazon and refers to the dried starchy pulp of the processed cassava root. Tapioca is used as a thickener and in pudding.

Members of the Yanomami carry cassava, also called manioc, out of Brazil's Amazon rain forest.

Indians on the Caribbean island of Hispaniola served Columbus a flat, tortilla-like bread made from cassava flour. Convinced of the superiority of their own familiar wheat breads, the Spanish never seemed to have a good word for cassava, which they considered too bland.

One quality of cassava that did impress the Spanish was its remarkable resilience and durability. It was easy to grow and harvest, and the flatbread made from its flour lasted as long as two years and did not decay in transit. Like Andean chuño, cassava bread was an ideal food for military rations. But cassava also figured in cultural tragedies. Some of the Arawak Indians killed themselves by drinking the poisonous liquid of the bitter cassava root rather than live under the harsh rule of the Spanish colonizers.

In the late 1500s, Portuguese slave traders carried cassava from Brazil, their colony in South America, to the west coast of central Africa. There the Portuguese traded cassava for slaves, feeding them processed cassava on the crowded slave ships returning to Brazil. Cassava spread fairly rapidly throughout central Africa in an area that includes modern-day Cameroon, Gabon, Congo, the Democratic Republic of the Congo (Zaire), and Angola. The Portuguese may also have introduced cassava to the island of Madagascar off Africa's southeastern coast and to India in the 1700s, although

In the Yanomami lands, cooks make flat bread from cassava flour using methods that date back hundreds of years.

the plant's arrival in Asia has not been well documented.

At about the same time, cassava traveled with the Spanish to their colony in the Philippines and from there to Southeast Asia. In modern times, Thailand has become a major Southeast Asian exporter of cassava, sending out tons of tapioca for puddings and for thickeners.

1,500-Ton Tapioca Pudding Nearly Sinks Ocean Liner

CARDIFF, WALES. For a while today, the biggest tapioca pudding in the world threatened to split the seams of a Swiss freighter, but a dock official said firemen and the ship's crew finally got things under control. The official said dockworkers were unloading the 12,165-ton *Cassarate*, which a fire chief had earlier called a "huge tapioca time bomb."

Firemen earlier controlled the fire, which started in timber stacked in the upper holds 25 days ago at sea. The crew kept the smoldering timber dampened until the ship docked here late Tuesday. But the water from the [ship's] hoses seeped down to the lower holds, where 1,500 tons of tapioca from Thailand were stored. The water swelled the tapioca. Then the heat from the flames started to cook the sticky mess.

The swelling tapioca—enough to serve a million plates—could buckle the ship's steel plates, fire chiefs warned. The plan is to load the gluey mess onto a fleet of trucks and dispose of it. One report said there was enough to fill 500 trucks. But where do you dump 500 truckloads of tapioca pudding?

(*Capital Times*, Madison, Wisconsin, September 14, 1972)

A Global Root

Some scientists estimate that more than 500 million people worldwide—including tropical Africa, the Amazon region of South America, and many parts of Southeast Asia—rely on the starchy cassava root for a large percentage of their carbohydrate **calories.** Cassava usually makes up one-sixth of the total daily calories consumed by the average person on the island of Madagascar and in African countries such as Ghana, Nigeria, Liberia, the Democratic Republic of the Congo, Uganda, Tanzania, and Mozambique. In times of drought, Africans eat even more cassava, a plant that can tolerate limited amounts of rain.

*We thank the almighty God
For giving us cassava.
We hail thee cassava,
The great cassava.*

*You grow in poor soils,
You grow in rich soils.
You grow in gardens,
You grow in farms.*

*You are easy to grow.
Children can plant you,
Women can plant you,
Everybody can plant you.*

*We must sing for you
Great cassava, we must sing.
We must not forget thee,
The great one.*

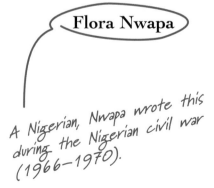

Flora Nwapa

A Nigerian, Nwapa wrote this during the Nigerian civil war (1966–1970).

From its beginnings in Central and South America, cassava has made the rounds. Vietnamese farmers dry cassava on mats *(top)*, and a Ugandan family make cut-up cassava part of their daily meal *(above)*.

Easy-Growing, Easy-Going Cassava

A young child who jams a stick in the ground, waters it, and hopes (usually in vain) to see something grow, would be delighted with the cassava. It grows exactly like that. If you live in the tropics, you can stick some woody cassava stems in the ground, water them, and watch buds and leaves form. Within a year, the mature cassava plant stands tall, sometimes waving its fingerlike leaves as high as 10 feet. Underground the roots swell up to produce many long, thick, brown-skinned tuberous growths. To harvest cassava, farmers lop off the tops of the foliage, then pull out the stumps and their attached roots by hand or by machine.

Cassava farmers often intercrop their fields with bananalike plantains, soybeans or mung beans, or even peanuts. Intercropping reduces the yield of any one crop but increases its ability to withstand pests and disease, thereby producing more food in total from one piece of land.

Most of the global cassava-eating population live in small villages, where planters typically have no extra money for irrigation equipment or fertilizers. For these people, the cassava plant's most valuable assets are its ability to produce under drought conditions and its tolerance of poor soils. Tropical areas of Africa and India, for example, receive plenty of sunshine and rainfall during annual wet seasons but are quite dry during the rest of the year. The cassava plant's leafy tops provide benefits beyond food. They shade the soil around each plant, thus discouraging weeds. When the plant's profuse leaves drop, they create natural fertilizer in the form of **organic matter**.

Cassava plants grow from woodlike stems into tall plants with thin trunks and leafy tops.

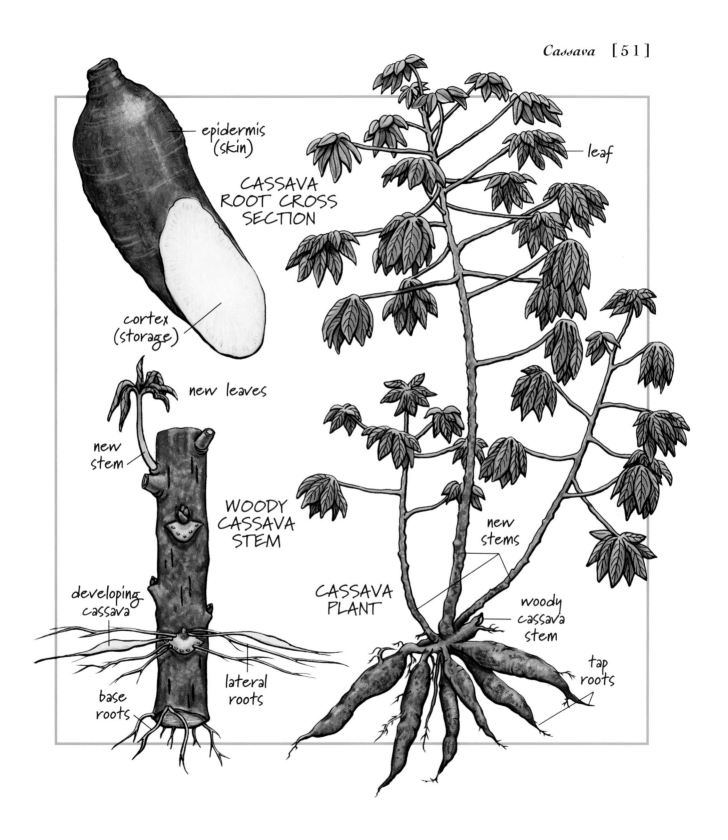

epidermis (skin)

CASSAVA ROOT CROSS SECTION

cortex (storage)

leaf

new leaves

new stem

WOODY CASSAVA STEM

developing cassava

base roots

lateral roots

CASSAVA PLANT

new stems

woody cassava stem

tap roots

Processing and Bringing Cassava to Market

Cassava roots provide bulk calories and keep well in the ground. Village bakers in many parts of the world depend on the root as a prime ingredient in long-lasting prepared foods such as bread. But cassava plants do have some drawbacks. After they are harvested, the roots rot quickly. This means that farmers usually haul fresh cassava directly to local markets, where the roots are sold within a day or two. In Kerala, India, women farmers commonly walk to market from their fields carrying cassava roots in baskets on

Among the daily chores of many African women is pounding cassava with a mortar (the bowl) and pestle (the stick) to make flour.

To Your Health!

The cassava root is all starch, with virtually no protein, although its leaves do contain protein and vitamins. In countries where people depend on cassava for the bulk of their daily calories, many people eat the cooked leaves of cassava along with the roots for a well-balanced meal.

Protein is vital to human and plant life. In fact, along with fats and carbohydrates, protein is one of the three major food groups that provide energy to the body. (Plants generate protein from elements in the air and in the soil.) Protein is a major part of human muscles, hair, nails, skin, eyes, and internal organs. Protein also helps fight infections and is necessary for growth. Good sources of protein include fish, poultry, meat, eggs, milk, beans, and nuts.

their heads. These women then sell the roots directly to the consumer or to a shopkeeper.

In parts of West Africa and South America—where the growing areas can be far from towns—distributors may contract with farmers for a certain amount of cassava each day. The distributors truck the roots to market and sell the cassava for the grower, taking a cut of the selling price for themselves and passing the rest back to the farmer.

To remove the poisonous content of cassava, villagers laboriously grate the roots into bowls and then let the plant's liquid drain. One traditional drainage method is to place the grated cassava in a mesh bag or tube. The liquid drips out from the bottom of the container, and the starchy substance that remains is used for flour. Boiling up the liquid produces a sticky sauce that can be safely eaten as well. Large-scale processors rely on mechanized graters and big settling tanks to extract the poison from cassava roots. Scientists have developed new varieties of cassava so that consumers can simply peel, cut up, and boil the root for a safe meal. Just remember never to eat a cassava root raw!

In Thailand, a major cassava exporter, production and processing are mechanized affairs. Cassava chips for animal feed, for example, are produced from locally made chipping machines. In undeveloped areas of Brazil, Nigeria, and other countries that depend on cassava as a major food source, the

In Thailand, where cassava growing is a commercial enterprise, workers wear protective masks during the harvesting process. The finished product will be used as cattle feed.

labor is very low-tech and is performed primarily by women. In fact, more than half of Nigeria's officially employed women are cassava processors. They are poorly paid and toil in hazardous work environments. The women who peel or grate the acidic root suffer burns and other skin ailments. To ensure healthier working conditions for these people, some cassava processors are providing better ventilation for the processing sheds and improved protective clothing and goggles.

Daily Fare

Several African and Asian dishes include cassava. A favorite in Rwanda, Africa, is mashed red beans and cassava meal. Liberians and other West Africans like *gari foto*—onions, tomatoes, cassava meal, and eggs—and *fufu*, cassava dumplings covered with spicy greens, meat, or fish stew. In Thailand cooks coat fish, shrimp, and squid with tapioca starch or flour before frying. Ground finer than cornstarch, tapioca also appears in many Asian recipes as a thickener for sauces. In Kerala, India, families eat fish with sliced, boiled cassava.

The cassava flatbread that Columbus tasted hundreds of years ago is still widely eaten in the Caribbean. Puerto Rican cooks make a vegetarian chili called *chili de yuca* from cassava and white beans. In Central America, Guatemalans enjoy a cassava soufflé. Folks in

(*Left*) In Ghana, West Africa, children share a meal of fufu with fish. (*Above*) A Brazilian farmer cuts up cassava to make tapioca.

Dig In!

Using a swift motion, a Vietnamese woman slices a cassava into small pieces before the drying process begins.

FAROFA (TOASTED MANIOC MEAL)
(1—2 servings)

4 tablespoons butter
1—1½ cups manioc flour
¼ cup water or milk

Melt the butter in a skillet over medium heat. Add the manioc flour and stir constantly until it turns golden brown. The flour will absorb all the butter first and will look like a mixture of pellets and loose flour. Just keep stirring, and it will eventually turn into something that looks like peanut butter. Slowly add the water or milk to get the consistency you want. Serve in a small ceramic bowl. You might want to top the farofa with raisins, prunes, fried bacon or sausage, cashew nuts, chopped olives, or sliced bananas.

Manioc flour, the main ingredient of farofa, can be found in large natural-foods stores and in Asian markets.

Using an underground oven, this Tahitian woman has made tapioca pudding, which she's placing on a serving dish for dinner.

Peru, South America, eat a rich dish made with a thick cheese sauce, cassava, and hot red and green chili peppers. *Yuca frita* from neighboring Colombia is simply french-fried cassava. Prominent on the dessert menu for the crew of the U.S. space shuttle *Columbia* in 1996 was tapioca pudding, an old-fashioned dessert that may be making a comeback.

It's a Fact!

Minute Tapioca—a cassava product introduced by the Whitman Grocery Company in Boston, Massachusetts, in 1894—was initially made by a local woman named Susan Stavers. She obtained cassava roots from South America and zipped them through her coffee grinder to get tapioca granules. The name "Minute" honored not the speed with which the dish could be prepared but the legendary Minutemen, the farmer-soldiers who held off British troops at the battles of Lexington and Concord in 1775 at the start of the American Revolution.

High-Tech Cassava

Used much in the same way as potato starch, cassava starch is increasingly attractive to a major Dutch potato-starch company in the Netherlands that has begun adding cassava-starch factories to its holdings. Cassava can also be a source of fuel alcohol. Researchers are experimenting further with the plant to see if its stalks can be burned to power the distillation boilers that turn the roots into fuel.

Researchers are also working to fight the mealybugs and tiny insects called green mites that attack and kill cassava plants. The mealybug was first identified in the Democratic Republic of the Congo in 1973. In its native habitat of Paraguay, South America, the mealybug was kept in check by its natural enemies, one of which is a type of wasp. But in Africa, where the cassava is not a native plant, there were no such enemies. Working from the International Institute of Tropical Agriculture (IITA) in Nigeria, Swiss scientist Dr. Hans Herren introduced mealybug wasps into Africa, a move that effectively halted the devastation of cassava plants in 30 African countries within seven years. In 1995 Dr. Herren won the World Food Prize, an award sponsored by the World Food Prize Foundation, for his outstanding work.

As for the green mites, IITA scientists in Benin, Africa, discovered another mite that found green mites tasty. Other researchers are working to alter the actual genetic make-up of the cassava plant so they can develop varieties with more protein in the root, higher productivity from each plant, and greater overall resistance to disease and insect attack.

You may be starting to understand that food growing is an international enterprise. A global community of scientists, plant breeders, and growers often work together to solve problems connected with the food we eat. But it is also a local activity, involving a range of people such as farmers, truckers, processors, and salespeople whom we seldom think of when we head out to buy food.

IITA scientists hope new clones of cassava will improve the plant's protein levels and resistance to disease and drought.

Carrots
[*Daucus carota*]

We associate carrots with bunnies and good eyesight (and maybe with soggy cafeteria salads we'd rather not think about). The vitamin A in carrots is vital to normal, healthy eyes. Some of us prefer the orange roots crispy cold, thinly sliced, and raw. A member of the parsley family, carrots are one of the world's oldest plant foods.

Originating in Afghanistan, the carrot traveled westward to the region of the Mediterranean Sea. By about 500 B.C., Greek writers were mentioning carrots, but we don't know how the carrot made its way to the Mediterranean nor exactly when. In fact, the carrot was not a big favorite among the Greeks, who named the vegetable *karoton*. They mainly used the root for its juice, which seemed to ease stomach ailments. At that time, people could choose from among purple, yellow, and even white varieties of the plant. The orange carrot we are familiar with was developed much later.

Pretty much the entire carrot—from its crunchy orange flesh to its long stems and lacy leaves—is edible and full of nutrition.

A cure for asthma. Live for a fortnight on boiled carrots only.

—John Wesley

For cartoon lovers, the carrot's most famous supporter is Bugs Bunny.

Arab traders probably carried the carrot westward from Afghanistan into Europe. By the 800s, the Frankish emperor Charlemagne was urging his subjects to grow more carrots. But whether they did or not is lost in history. The Flemish people of northern Belgium introduced carrots, as well as parsnips, to England in 1558. Starting with a mutant variety of carrot, the Flemings probably bred and refined the orange root we associate with Bugs Bunny's favorite treat.

Spanish conquistadores of the 1500s are said to have been the first to plant carrots in the Americas. They raised the roots on the island of Margarita, which lies off the coast of Venezuela in South America. By 1609 English settlers in Jamestown, Virginia, were growing carrots and their root pals, parsnips and turnips.

It's a Fact!

Queen Anne ruled Great Britain from 1702 to 1714 and was renowned for her lace making. The story goes that one day Queen Anne and her ladies-in-waiting were admiring the wild carrots growing in the royal garden. The queen challenged her ladies to create lace as delicate as that of the carrot flower. As is usual with queens, Anne's lace won, and the wild carrot flower has been called Queen Anne's lace ever since.

Queen Anne's lace

Sold by Dutch merchants in Amsterdam in the early 1600s, the Hoorn was one of the first varieties of carrot that colonists brought to North America. This type of carrot was named for the Dutch community from which it came (Hoorn, Netherlands) and soon was known in North America as the Early Dutch Horn. Other varieties have names tied to locales, too. For example, a carrot bred in Danvers, Massachusetts, in 1870 was known as the Danvers. The modern-day Nantes carrot came originally from Nantes, France.

Carrot Cultivation

China grows more carrots than any other country, with the United States second in world production. California produces 80 percent of all U.S. carrots. Florida, Michigan, and Washington also rank as top carrot-growing states.

Like many other vegetable crops in China, carrots are cultivated with much hand labor, especially when it comes to watering and to applying organic fertilizers. Chinese farmers usually intercrop carrots with other food plants in small raised beds (plots) that are usually no more than six feet wide. Irrigation furrows along each side of the raised plots bring water to the crops.

Nearly all the major commercial carrot-growing areas in the United States rely on machines to plant and harvest carrots. There's even a machine called a bed-former to create a wide platform where the seeds are placed in two-row groupings. Two to four months after planting, the carrots are mature. Two-row harvesters chop the long stems and fernlike greenery off each plant, dig out the carrot, and shoot the carrot into a truck moving alongside the harvester.

Commercial carrots differ in size and shape depending on their use. Fresh market carrots are about nine inches in length, the longest of all commercial varieties. Three-inch baby carrots, a specialty item, are the

This early French illustration depicts some of the different colors of carrots. The French were instrumental in popularizing carrots throughout Europe.

Dig In!

Planting carrots in your home garden is usually a by-hand operation. The tiny seeds prefer fine, well-prepared soil. And because carrots are roots that grow downward, the soil beneath them has to be loose. First, buy a packet of carrot seeds at your local garden center or hardware store. Prepare your carrot garden in the spring by loosening the soil with a shovel or hoe. With a trowel (a gardener's hand tool resembling a small shovel), dig shallow furrows about 1/2-inch deep. Sow the seeds according to the directions on the package. Keep the soil moist but don't spray the planted area too hard. Young carrots hate to fight their way through heavy soil. Tiny carrot greens should start to appear approximately one or two weeks after planting. As they grow, thin out the carrots by pulling up a few plants in each row so they don't become overcrowded. You can even wash off the dirt and nibble some carrots as you go!

shortest. For canned and frozen diced carrots, commercial growers raise processing carrots, which are wider and an inch or two shorter than the market varieties.

Crunchy, Sweet, and Orange

A low-key vegetable, carrots have always done well in a supporting role. Mixed with other foods such as beef and vegetable stew, spaghetti sauce, and minestrone, carrots add natural sugars to the mix. The Chinese, who eat a huge range of vegetables, are said to find carrots flavorless. They add carrots to dishes purely for a splash of color. The French cook sliced carrots to perfection in chicken broth with garlic and sprigs of herbs

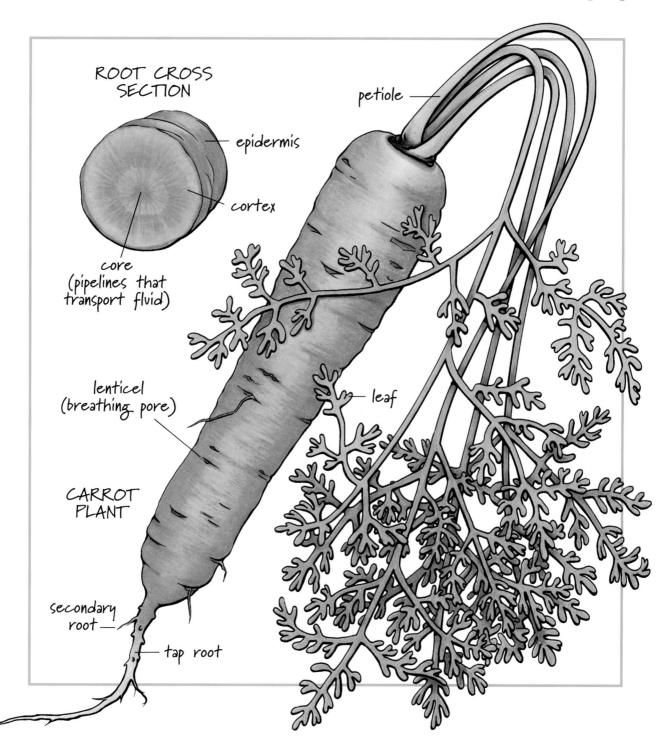

ROOT CROSS
SECTION

epidermis

cortex

core
(pipelines that
transport fluid)

petiole

leaf

lenticel
(breathing pore)

CARROT
PLANT

secondary
root

tap root

Dr. Phil Simon shows off a bunch of Beta III carrots, which are high in carotene, a substance that converts to vitamin A. Lack of this vitamin—which helps to maintain healthy bones, teeth, skin, eyes, and internal systems—ranks among the world's most serious nutritional problems.

It's a Fact!

Containing more sugar than any other vegetable except beets, carrots are also an excellent source of vitamin A. For healthy eyes and skin, humans need at least 5,000 international units (IUs) of vitamin A every day. One cup of carrots has more than 20,000 IUs of vitamin A—that's more than four times the daily requirement!

such as parsley and tarragon. Ginger and sour cream are featured in a preparation from Turkey called carrot *plaki*. Polish chefs prepare carrots in a thick cream sauce with dill. The carrot cake familiar in North America derives from a German recipe for carrot nut bread.

It's a Bird, It's a Plane, It's Super Carrot!

Dr. Phil Simon, a plant scientist at the University of Wisconsin, is developing a super carrot in cooperation with the U.S. Department of Agriculture. Dubbed Beta III, the carrot contains three to five times the amount of vitamin A found in an average carrot. Beta III was bred especially for growing in developing countries where severe vitamin A deficiency leaves hundreds of thousands of people blind each year.

Dig In!

ENSALADA MIXTA (4 servings)

SALAD
2 medium carrots, peeled and sliced diagonally
2 medium beets, peeled and cubed
1 medium cucumber, peeled, seeded, and cubed
DRESSING
6 tablespoons vegetable oil
3 tablespoons fresh lemon or lime juice
2 tablespoons chopped fresh cilantro
1 small garlic clove, minced or pressed
salt and pepper to taste

Microwave the beets and carrots until tender but not overcooked. This could take about 10 minutes. Be sure to test for tenderness with a fork. Mix the steamed vegetables in a large bowl and add the cucumbers. Combine the dressing ingredients. Pour the dressing over the veggies and toss lightly. Chill in refrigerator for two hours. Toss lightly again before serving.

Cilantro looks sort of like a bunch of parsley but with bigger leaves.

Turnips, Beets, and Radishes

[*Brassica rapa, Beta vulgaris,* and *Raphanus sativus*]

This threesome, underground root veggies all, has not made the headlines the way other roots and tubers have. But we eat them and enjoy them for themselves. Turnips, beets, and radishes are less important to human survival than other staple underground crops. In addition, less is known about them. Nevertheless, they fill worthy roles as accent foods, as solid stew ingredients, or as side dishes.

Last but not least are turnips, beets, and radishes. Along with other second stringers like rutabagas, these three form a less flashy tier of root vegetables that nevertheless appear in lots of soups, stews, and salads.

A man may feel thankful, heartily thankful, over a dish of plain mutton with turnips. . . .

—Charles Lamb

Beets, emollient, nutritive and relaxing.

—John Arbuthnot

An old radish is a worthless radish.

—Waverley Root

Turnips Keep Turning Up

Before potatoes were abundant beyond South America, turnips were everyday staples, particularly in Europe during the Middle Ages (A.D. 500–1500). The origins of the turnip are vague, but it may have come from northeastern Europe or Asia many thousands of years ago.

Thriving in a cold, damp climate, turnips were the food of Europe's poor people, the majority of the population. For this reason, wealthy Europeans looked down on the turnip for hundreds of years. Yet records show that the Duke of Orléans gave an all root-vegetable dinner in France in 1690. At some undetermined point in history, the less nutritious turnip gave up its role as everyday vegetable to the spud and ceased being a staple food.

In 1730 Charles "Turnip" Townshend, a British politician, imported Dutch-grown turnips. He wanted to see if his livestock could survive in good health

Charles Townshend (inset), a noted British politician of the 1700s, resigned from his duties in 1730 and devoted himself to agricultural improvements, including the cultivation of turnips. This work earned him the nickname "Turnip" Townshend. More than 200 years later, British sheep were grazing in a turnip field in northwestern England.

In Myanmar (formerly Burma), farmers bring cartloads of turnips to a wholesale market.

throughout the winter on a diet of turnips. Hay and other traditional winter **fodder** were expensive for farmers to raise and tricky to store. Most people kept to the ancient custom of killing their livestock in the fall. But this practice left families with too much meat. In an era before refrigeration, the meat quickly spoiled or had to be saturated in expensive spices to remain edible. Townshend proved that with turnips, which were easy to grow and to store, farmers could fatten cattle through the winter and slaughter the animals only as needed.

Farmers still feed turnips to livestock. In Great Britain, farmers invite sheep and pigs right into the turnip fields. And of course, people in Great Britain, Germany, Poland, Russia, the Czech Republic, and many other places continue to eat turnips, as well as their green tops, much as they always did — mixed and mashed with potatoes or tossed into soups and stews.

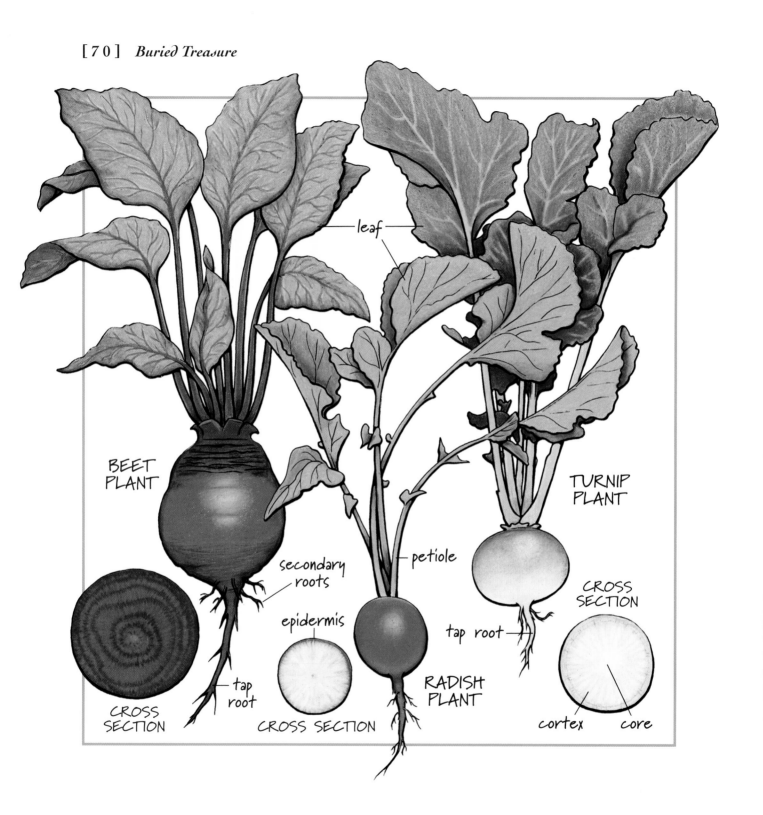

BEET
PLANT

leaf

secondary
roots

epidermis

petiole

TURNIP
PLANT

CROSS
SECTION

CROSS
SECTION

tap
root

tap root

RADISH
PLANT

CROSS SECTION

cortex   core

Planting and Harvesting

Farmers and home gardeners commonly plant turnips, beets, and radishes. They're easy to raise because they grow fast and are usually ready to harvest within only eight weeks of planting. Farmers plant all three root crops in the early spring, since the plants like cool weather and can usually tolerate frost. In the United States, top radish-growing areas are Florida, California, and Ohio. Wisconsin and New York lead the nation in producing table beets, while turnips are grown chiefly in the southern part of the country.

Because turnips, beets, and radishes grow quickly and don't mind cool weather, they are favorite choices for growers in some of the world's less hospitable climates. *(Left)* In Russia a truck dumps a load of beets picked from a collective farm (a large estate where farmers share the work and the profits). *(Above)* A woman in Poland has gotten good results from her turnip harvest.

Beet You to the Punch

The beet is a Mediterranean plant, possibly from Italy, although some food historians think beets may have derived from a wild plant stock with a far broader reach. Table beets, or beets grown as vegetables, are a good source of protein and minerals. Like carrots, beets are very high in sugar, so farmers around the world plant sugar beets as a major source of commercial sugar.

Peoples in ancient Babylonia, Egypt, and Greece grew beets thousands of years ago. In the late 1700s, beets bred entirely for their sugar content began to attract attention in Europe. By 1812 Napoléon Bonaparte, emperor of France, had ordered French farmers to plant 70,000 acres of sugar beets. At war with Great Britain and much of Europe at this time, France faced shortages of sugar and other imported goods because of British blockades of French port cities. Further development of the sugar beet continued in Germany, where the white Silesian—the ancestor of all modern varieties of sugar beet—was born. Some 200 years later, Germany is one of the world's top producers of sugar beets, ranking third after France and Ukraine.

Beets also come in handy for their color. Beet juice is widely used to give processed foods the desirable

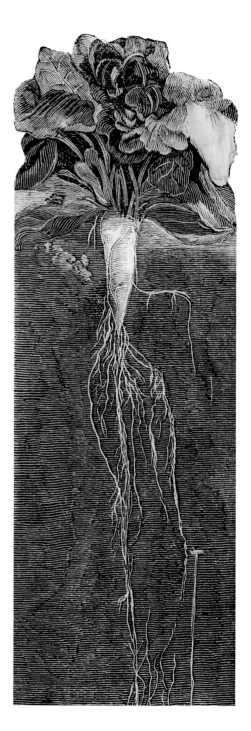

Fully grown sugar beets, one of the world's main sources of sugar, have a cone-shaped white root that eventually thins to a taproot. Stretching into the soil, the taproot can get water from deep underground sources.

It's a Fact!

Sugar beets provide about 40 percent of the world's commercial sugar. Minnesota and North Dakota are among the top growers of sugar beets in the United States.

The table beet's root, as well as its green leaves, are full of calcium and iron.

pink or red coloration otherwise achieved with artificial red dyes. Ukrainians use the deep red flesh of the beet to dye their famous Easter eggs, too.

The people of Ukraine and Russia, among others, have created a variety of memorable beet dishes. The most famous are beet salad and a soup called borscht, both made supremely delicious by the addition of heavy cream or sour cream. Make a bowl of borscht yourself. It's easy!

Pass the Sugar, Please

Sugar beets, which contain a natural sugar called **sucrose,** are a common source of table sugar all over the world. The United States produces almost 8 million tons of sugar every year. About half of that comes from sugar beets raised on U.S. farms.

After farmers harvest their sugar beets, they ship the roots to processing plants where machines cut the beets into thin slices called cossettes. The cossettes are then soaked to release the sucrose. Workers purify the sugary liquid through heating and filtering processes. Then workers place the purified liquid in evaporator tanks to remove water, creating a thick, syrupy liquid. The syrup is heated, and sugar crystals begin to form. Workers place the syrup-crystal

Dig In!

BORSCHT
(4 servings)

2 large beets

1 onion
2 med. carrots
3 med. potatoes
2 T. olive oil

3 cups vegetable
broth
2 cups water
½ green pepper

¼ cabbage
1 tsp. lemon juice
½ cup sour cream
black pepper

Microwave washed beets on high for 12–15 minutes. Peel and thinly slice onions, carrots, and potatoes. Put with oil in large soup pot and sauté on medium until onions are clear. Add broth and bring to a boil. Cover pot and simmer until potatoes are soft (5–10 minutes). Remove from heat. Mash vegetables in pot. Add water. Cool beets in cold water, then peel and grate into soup pot. Slice green pepper and cabbage into thin strips and add to pot. Cook on medium for 5 minutes. Stir in lemon juice. Ladle soup into bowls. Top with a dollop of sour cream and some black pepper.

Borscht is a beet soup that can be served hot or cold.

mixture in a high-speed centrifuge machine, which spins fast to force the syrup to separate from the crystals. The raw-sugar crystals then go through a cycle of rinsing, filtering, evaporation, spinning, and drying to produce the processed white table sugar we buy at the local supermarket.

The Tangy Radish

Considered good appetite stimulators, radishes actually have very little food value. But they do add tang, texture, and crunch to meals. They also add color, coming in hues of white, lavender, red, and pink. Mentioned by

Chinese philosopher Confucius back in 479 B.C., radishes probably originated in China but are so ancient that their original ancestor is not known.

The ancient Greeks ate radishes as well as turnips and beets. One historian writes that the Greeks made vegetable sacrifices to the gods, carrying turnips on lead platters, beets on silver, and radishes on gold. In modern times, artists carve the long, **hybrid** radishes raised around the town of Oaxaca, Mexico, into elaborate, detailed sculptures for La Noche de los Rábanos (the Night of the Radishes). Each December 23, the carved radishes are displayed in Oaxaca's central square. The best carving wins a prize.

Crunch Food

The Belgians and the French eat radishes as a crisp summer treat, finely sliced on crusty bread spread with soft, white cheese. But radishes can hardly be considered daily fare anywhere except in China, home to dozens of radish varieties, and in Japan. Japan is known for the daikon radish, a hardy variety that can stay in the ground through the winter. Daikon radishes are planted in deep, loose soil. The long, white, curvy roots are harvested and hung to dry in the sun for at least two weeks before the daikon is ready for processing.

The Japanese prepare traditional meals that include a variety of small dishes.

An artist puts the finishing touches on his radish carving, which will be part of the festivities of the Night of the Radishes in Oaxaca, Mexico.

Tsukemono, or pickled vegetables, are often eaten after the rice—the mainstay of the Japanese meal. Of the pickled vegetables, the pickled daikon is said to be the number-one favorite in Japan.

Pickling came about to preserve fresh foods for winter consumption. Invented by a Japanese priest in the early 1600s, pickled daikon is easy to make. Picklers simply salt the radishes, place them in a barrel, and weight the lid with a heavy stone. Together the salt and the weighted lid force liquid from the radishes, which essentially pickle in their own juices. The result is a crisp, fresh-tasting vegetable treat.

To Your Health!

Daikon radishes dry by the roadside in Japan. The word *daikon* comes the Japanese words *dai*, meaning "big," and *kon*, meaning "root."

Radishes contain mostly water, so they are low in food value and calories. Turnips and beets, on the other hand, are good sources of the mineral potassium. Minerals are a basic part of the human body. Most minerals are in the bones, although some are found in blood and body tissues. Like vitamins, minerals help the body produce energy. Potassium, one of the most important minerals, helps to maintain healthy blood and nerve cells, to regulate the heartbeat, and to build muscles. Fish, whole grains, nuts, and many fresh fruits and vegetables—such as spinach, potatoes, bananas, and citrus fruits—are excellent sources of potassium.

Vitamins are natural compounds that come from foods. In small amounts, we need them inside our bodies to grow and stay healthy.

Glossary

calorie: A unit of measurement expressing the amount of heat produced by a food when it burns. Scientists use this information to determine how much energy a food provides when it is fully digested and used by the body.

domestication: Taming animals or adapting plants so they can safely live with or be eaten by humans.

eye: An undeveloped potato bud, or growing point, from which a new potato plant can sprout.

fodder: Hay, corn, vegetables, or other coarse food for cattle, sheep, and other livestock.

hybrid: The offspring of a pair of plants or animals of different species.

intercrop: To grow a variety of crops on the same piece of land, often by planting different crops in alternating rows.

organic matter: Dead plants and animals in various stages of rotting.

photosynthesis: The chemical process by which green plants make energy-producing carbohydrates. The process involves the reaction of sunlight to carbon dioxide, water, and nutrients within plant tissues.

staple crop: A food plant that is widely cultivated across a given region and used on a regular basis.

sucrose: A sugar that occurs naturally in most plants. The sucrose in sugarcane and sugar beets is used in making commercial sugars.

Further Reading

Hill, Lee Sullivan. *Farms Feed the World.* Minneapolis: Carolrhoda Books, 1997.

Hughes, Meredith Sayles. *The Great Potato Book.* New York: Macmillan and Co., 1987.

Inglis, Jane. *Proteins.* Minneapolis: Carolrhoda Books, 1993.

Johnson, Sylvia A. *Potatoes.* Minneapolis: Lerner Publications, 1984.

Johnson, Sylvia A. *Tomatoes, Potatoes, Corn, and Beans: How the Foods of the Americas Changed Eating around the World.* New York: Atheneum Books for Young Readers, 1997.

Nottridge, Rhoda. *Vitamins.* Minneapolis: Carolrhoda Books, 1993.

Root, Waverley. *Food.* New York: Simon & Schuster, 1980.

Sekido, Isamu. *Fruits, Roots, and Fungi.* Minneapolis: Lerner Publications, 1993.

Trager, James. *The Food Chronology.* New York: Henry Holt and Company, 1995.

Turner, Dorothy. *Potatoes.* Minneapolis: Carolrhoda Books, 1989.

A foodseller in Riga, the capital of Latvia, offers radishes and carrots among her wares.

Index

About the Authors

Meredith Sayles Hughes and Tom Hughes—a teacher/writer/lecturer team—are the authors of *The Great Potato Book* as well as several articles on other food-related topics. Meredith and Tom are also the founders of The FOOD Museum in Albuquerque, New Mexico. As part of their museum work, they have put together several exhibits about food for the Smithsonian and a variety of other institutions. Over the years, they have developed and presented a wide range of domestic and international lectures, workshops, trainings, and conferences about food. The Hughes make their home in Albuquerque.

Acknowledgments

For photographs and artwork: Steve Brosnahan, p. 5; TN State Museum, detail of a painting by Carlyle Urello, p. 7; Panos Pictures: © Sean Sprague, pp. 11, 52, 54 (right)/ © Jim Holmes, p. 19 (right)/ © Bruce Paton, pp. 43 (left), 57/ © Penny Tweedie, p. 49 (bottom)/ © John Miles, p. 50/ © Ron Giling, p. 53/ © Jean-Léo Dugast, p. 69; © John Phelan/DDB Stock Photo, p. 12; Corbis-Bettmann, pp. 13, 16 (right), 19 (left), 43 (right); Jamestown, Lib. of VA, p. 15; North Wind Picture Archives, pp. 16 (left), 32, 60 (right), 72; James F. Dill, ME Coop. Ext. Service, pp. 17, 23 (inset); Lib. of Congress, p. 18; © Masaharu Suzuki, p. 21; © William H. Allen, Jr., p. 22; Kenneth Chapman, ME Coop. Ext. Service, pp. 23 (left and top right); Ryan Farms, East Grand Forks, MN, p. 23 (bottom); © Inga Spence/DDB Stock Photo, p. 24; J. Wishnetsky/The Potato Museum, p. 25; Jeff Greenberg, pp. 27, 71 (left), 78; Kennedy Space Center, FL, p. 28; Walt/Louiseann Pietrowicz, pp. 29, 42, 65, 74; Steve Foley, pp. 31, 55 (right), 59, 67; Cameramann International, Ltd., pp. 33, 38, 56, 71 (right); © Nik Wheeler, p. 35; The Potato Museum, pp. 36, 61; NC Division of Archives & History, p. 37; © Victor Englebert, pp. 40, 46, 47, 54 (left); NC Dept. of Agriculture, p. 41; © Christine Osborne Pictures/MEP, p. 45; © Nevada Wier, pp. 49 (top), 55 (left); Hollywood Book & Poster, p. 60 (left); P. W. Simon, USDA, ARS, p. 64; Rural History Centre, University of Reading, p. 68 (both); Mary Altier, p. 73; © Robin J. Dunitz/DDB Stock Photo, p. 75; © Paul J. Buklarewicz, p. 76. Sidebar and back cover artwork by John Erste. All other artwork by Laura Westlund. Cover photo by Steve Foley and Rena Dehler.

For quoted material: p. 4, M. F. K. Fisher, *The Art of Eating* (New York: Macmillan Reference, 1990); p. 10, Sir Thomas Overbury, *The Overburian Characters* (Oxford: B. Blackwell, 1936); p. 30, William Shakespeare, *The Merry Wives of Windsor*; act 5, sc. 5, lines 17-18; p. 44, Richard Ligon, *A True and Exact History of the Island of Barbadoes* (London: Peter Parker, 1673); p. 49, Flora Nwapa, www.worldbank.org/html/cgiar/newsletter/mar96/4cas2.htm; p. 58, John Wesley, *Primitive Remedies* (Beverly Hills, CA: Woodbridge Press, 1973); p. 66 (top), Charles Lamb, *The Complete Works and Letters of Charles Lamb* (New York: Modern Library, 1935); p. 66 (middle), John Arbuthnot, *Practical Rules of Diet* (London: J. Tonson, 1732); p. 66 (bottom), Waverly Root, *Food* (New York: Simon & Schuster, 1980).

For recipes (some slightly adapted for kids): p. 29, Meredith Sayles Hughes, *I Can too Cook*. Peelings, no. 47 (Washington, D.C.: Potato Museum, 1986); p. 42, reprinted with permission from "Glazed Sweet Potatoes" in *The World in Your Kitchen* by Troth Wells. © 1993. Published by The Crossing Press: Freedom, CA; p. 55, www.maria-brazil.org/farofa/htm; p. 65, Moosewood Collective, *Sundays at Moosewood Restaurant* (New York: Simon & Schuster, 1990); p. 74, Gregory Plotkin and Rita Plotkin, *Cooking the Russian Way* (Minneapolis: Lerner Publications Company, 1986).